These poems are brilliant and dangerous. The opening poem, "Invisible Woman, Dancing," is the best protest poem of the decade. The speaker attends a party full of casual, good-intentioned racists and ableists. The ending of the poem is explosive. Constance Merritt shows incredible range – erotic poems to a wayward lover; blues lyrics so rhythmic I can nearly hear the guitar; and devotional poems that offer "this, you know, is love, is all, the end." *Blind Girl Grunt* is a major work by a major poet.

—Jillian Weise

Merritt's latest collection is a back in bend—bend in love, bend in prayer, and bend in anger. A Blues infiltrates these lines and stanzas, ready to sing and stay (as any devoted lover) through the long haul. And the haul here is a woman, her myriad contents, in medias res.

—CM Burroughs

Beyond their shared—and dazzling—immunity to taboos, the poems in Constance Merritt's fourth book are very different from each other. Different in form, from stern villanelles to get-drunk-on-them blues poems to wandering narratives. And they are different in their tones, with ruthless self-awareness next to sexy lullaby next to persuasive rage at being "unmoored and vanishing" beyond "the flag of whiteness." Even within single poems, tone is protean. "The Less Than Greater Than Blues" is goofily playful and also as blunt as blunt gets about the roots of the suffering we cause each other. The penultimate poem "Advent" shifts between a longing that intends to wreck and a longing that intends to redeem. In fact the book as a whole shifts between these longings. As do we. Merritt implicates us gently but without hesitation, wrapping us into the "brilliant skin, the ruinous eyes,/ the body poised in transit" that opens the collection and that judges and blesses, throughout it. *Blind Girl Grunt* is supple, and rigorous, and so surprising. It is vital.

—Taije Silverman

Other Books by Constance Merritt

Two Rooms

Blessings and Inclemencies

A Protocol for Touch

Blind Girl Grunt

Blind Girl Grunt

The Selected Blues Lyrics and Other Poems

Constance Merritt

HEADMISTRESS PRESS

ISBN-13:978-0997914917
ISBN-10:0997914912

Cover art Robert Delaunay, *Premier Disque* (1913). Public Domain.
Cover & book design by Mary Meriam

These poems first appeared in the following journals:
Lavender Review: "Less Than Greater Than Blues"
Prairie Schooner: "Invisible Woman, Dancing," "A Good Day," "Voc Rehab," "Lonely in the House of Love," "Writing in the Dark," "The Green Revolution," "Meditation on a Theme Suggested by Dr. Trellou Joseph Pond," "so much depends / upon," "Parody/ Prayer," and "Ephemeroptera Hymn"

PUBLISHER
Headmistress Press
60 Shipview Lane
Sequim, WA 98382
Telephone: 917-428-8312
Email: headmistresspress@gmail.com
Website: headmistresspress.blogspot.com

Contents

Invisible Woman Dancing

Lonely in the House of Love

On Civil Disobedience

Blind Girl Grunt: The Selected Blues Lyrics

Song of Her Dark Hair

Grace Notes

for M
everything & always

Invisible Woman Dancing

Invisible Woman, Dancing

All Hallows Eve, Sweet Briar College, 2003

I came as a ghost to the party,
no costume required, I only had to wear
the brilliant skin, the ruinous eyes,
the body poised in transit, unwriting
the myth of sex. I came as a ghost
to the party, though we pretended
not to notice a palpable hovering
in the interstices of conversations,
a presence so insubstantial
eyes passed through it, hands
reached through air, bodies jostled
on the dance floor and never felt a thing.

Still, some there were haunted,
drawn away from the company,
its clenched knots of desperate clever banter,
to contemplate the thinnest air
as if, despite themselves,
they heard and heeded a ghostly tongue;
their bodies swayed in answer.
Staring into that void they glimpsed themselves,
turned back, shuddering, to the masquerade.

I came as a ghost to the party
against my better judgment
at the persistent, earnest
urging of my friends, as if
a ghost had friends when they hoist
the flag of whiteness and huddle there
under purity and privilege, surrender—fatal—
the furious, frailer, darker parts
of themselves. Recently they had rallied
to kiss the ass of a black man who had accomplished
admirable things—though most there had not read
them or only read a story,
as pleasantly exotic and sweetly soothing

as those wonderful spirituals
about wading in the water and summertime.
So extravagant was their ardor
that I, a member of his tribe,
could not get near him or have one word.
Still, I know he saw me, sitting there, tense, alone,
before his lecture, unmoored and vanishing
in the cocktail Hell before his dinner—
did not only see, but recognized a kindred ache.
The first and second and third rule of thumb,
the commentator said, is do not scare
the white people. And so we stand apart,
raise no specters of over-educated house
niggers breeding insurrections, mustering
ghost armies of strangers, lepers, freaks,
the wretched of the earth, furious,
innumerable and not afraid to die.

I came as a ghost to the party.
You didn't wear a costume, someone said.
I came as an activist, I replied,
modeling my black ACLU t-shirt,
Lady Liberty emblazoned down my front,
at my back, a litany of rights.
I might have said the costume's in the eye.
You will weave for me a shroud
and I will walk among you like a ghost,
mask of the red death, memento mori.

Blind with pride and rage
(I will ask no one for help), I quit the place,
leave the lake behind, the band's god-awful
din, the strafing voices—the rent
in the world's fabric miraculously healed
by my going. The dark deserted road
is unfamiliar, its grade, its curves,
the woods casting shadows from either side,
but any path is right that leads away.
I lose my way, keep going, going,

deeper into the maze, finally turn back.
Returned, the band's on break;
they've put a mix tape in.
I dance like one possessed, furious grace.
When strangers, not of this place,
say a quick goodnight, I run after,
take me with you, I say.

A solid hand upon my solid knee, warm hands
returning the pressure of my warm hand—
two women rescue me, deliver me—
ghost in the machine
once more human girl—home
with promises of brunch and company
they will or will not keep.
No matter. I lock the door
and slide the chain, rest back against
the frame, breathing relief.
May they all die horribly in a boathouse fire.
The malediction takes me by surprise.
I say it once again with clear intent:
May they all die horribly in a boathouse fire.
These words be kerosene, dry wood, locked doors, a match.

Lonely in the House of Love

A Good Day

If comes bliss after years of numb
and loneliness, what missives might
one pen from the peaks of ardor?

I have been with you all day:

over unsweet tea and barbecue
and the ditsy, DIY,
southern sweetheart waitress
who (bless her heart) plunks
our drinks down out of reach
and has to be asked twice (at least!)
for everything; she sparks
us into laughter (for risen
from our first love
what could spoil our mood?)
and easy camaraderie
with our fellow under-served,
french-fry-denied patrons;
down the aisles of the garden
center at Lowe's, hefting bags
of potting soil and mulch,
choosing your first hand tools,
flower food and flowers—pansies
and Dianthus (the ones called pinks)
to plant along with yellow trumpet
daffodils (surplus from my garden)
in graduated terracotta-colored
plastic pots flanking your front door;
to Target for tomorrow's party at work,
a baby shower for a soon-to-be
grandma for which you see
no need, but nevertheless buy
a twenty-dollar gift, a tin of nuts,
wrapping paper and bow;
and finally home
to plant our flowers,
talk to family on the phone

(my mom, your sister),
a couple of beers, a dinner of quiche,
desultory baseball, then early to bed.
I have been with you all day,
but how I've missed you,
skin on skin, drowning in a kiss.

Lullaby

Wring from me
pleasures and cries;
unwind the spring,
unloose the sluices
frozen fast inside
of me these years.

Lay me down
and lay to rest at last
these frigid fears
of something wrong;
draw me out and out;
go slow and deep and long.

Bold sun, burnish my skin;
roll and soften and mold
in your strong hands
my silly putty;
bring forth, insatiable
and unashamed, a brand new woman.

Let summer swell the flower;
let bees fatten the hive.
Layer by patient layer
pare sweetness to its core.
Lay your lovely mouth there,
gently sipping, sucking hard,
'til, like wine or mother's milk,
the heavy honey flow.

Voc Rehab

Once my hands, dispirited, unemployed,
hung about the house like down-sized
corporate jocks or hormone hopped-up teens,
out of sorts with the world
and from themselves irreconcilably estranged.

Desperate for something to do,
they contemplated crochet,
arts & crafts, brain surgery,
complicated recipes; coveted
the comfort of a ritual:
a book of old-fashioned matches,
cigarette paper, tobacco pouch, or
the finer arts of crime: sneakthief,
counterfeiter, pickpocket, safebreak,
but in the end could only muster
prodigious mastery of remote control
and the shameful, short-lived solace
of compulsive cuticle mutilation.

Now, cocooned inside your Ford Explorer,
our forearms kiss on the console,
palm to palm, our fingers intertwine,
graze knuckles, caress the little crotches;
thumbs firmly knead calluses and pads,
trace the rivers flowing through the hand:
lifeline, loveline, destiny,
the intricate lacework at the wrist;
the smooth back of the hand
shivers with a kiss—
epigastric rising, flippy-do.

More than the quenchless skin
it is the hands' insatiable hunger
that astounds me again and again:

the hover and perch and glide
of your fluttering small bird hands,
the dawn song I wake to,
is stilled only by sleep.

I am making of your body
the most intricate map imaginable;
moment by moment, my diligent fingers work
at loosening the hard knots of your living,
unriddling every last secret
from your skin's obscure Braille,
inscribing its ample surface
with the epic of forty years.

Still Life: Stone Wall, Bloodied Head

Into thin air
my beloved vanished.

I never guessed her going,
had no time to prepare.

One morning, breakfast ready,
I went to wake her;

she asked if I would lie with her awhile.
I did. As yet nothing had changed.

After breakfast, we loaded up the car
and hit the road.

At first her dog was fussy,
but he soon settled down.

Crossing North Carolina she grew distant,
said she wasn't feeling quite herself.

After a late lunch we ran into heavy traffic;
we wound our way to Georgia along the backroads.

We made it home alive.
Only not we, but each of us, alone.

Time passed slowly:
hours, days, a lifetime.

I pined for her, for us.
I wondered where she'd gone,

tried to think what I'd done wrong,
how to put things right.

I wanted to speak soft words to her,
to lure her back by touch.

Instead I shrank away;
the stranger in her place gave me chills.

My resolve to track her
came, but late.

Where are you? Remember me?
I called and called and called.

As if each present moment
must hold its past somewhere,

as if our loves weren't all too often
lighter than thinnest air.

Lonely in the House of Love,

who can measure the length of a day,
the weight of an hour,
the ounces of salt in a week's worth of tears—
every vow unraveled by silence,
every good gift withdrawn,
hope's long road narrowed to this
last night in a strange bed:
one of you clenched against the cold and sobbing,
the other steeling herself against compassion
or simply indifferent or sleeping;
both intent on morning, the mercy of departure?

Pantoum

I longed to be the perfect wife:
I folded clothes, I made the bed;
I wore my soul out on my sleeve,
and took to heart the things you said.

I folded clothes; I made the bed.
I took you to my coral reef.
I took to heart the things you said.
We were happy beyond belief.

I rocked you on my coral reef.
I planted flowers, massaged your head.
We were happy beyond belief.
I hung on every word you said.

On Civil Disobedience

What Gets Lost

Love gets lost, lives get lost when leaders lie and stay the course and love their pride more than the lives of the poor and lost. The way gets lost. The point gets lost. I get lost in thought, in loneliness, in cyberspace. The way gets lost. No maps to lead us on or back. Lives get lost, here and faraway. Love gets lost. Second by second our lives are lost; second by second we throw life away—wasting love, wasting time as if one could save one's breath. Death gets lost when life is death. The way gets lost. And if I lost door keys or houses, my mother's watch, how would that compare? Faith gets lost. The way gets lost. Daily we accept the toll of young lives lost. We drink it down with morning coffee; we butter our bread. We do not scream or go mad. Which means our minds are already lost. We lose the power to awake. We lose the grace of dreams. Are we losing sleep? Or are we sleeping still?

Lives are lost. The way is lost. We throw the brightest pearls away. The maps are wrong; the maps are torn; they will not lead us forward or back or anywhere beyond the quagmire we've been sinking in—how many years? The way is lost. Truth is lost. Our wills are nailed to some ungodly cross. We hang there calm; we do not flail. The day is lost. Soon another night; another week; another year. The way is lost. My faith is lost. They have closed down the office of the lost and found, and I don't even know who they are. We are they; they is us. It was beautiful the office of the lost and found.

Writing in the Dark

What was the light like—carnival or massacre?
Leaves shown like spun gold in the live oak canopy.

And these pale attendings—angels, physicians, witnesses?
Brimstones, orangetips, sulfurs, whites.

A murder of crows rowed in until the sky was a blue eye blackened.
Someone had forced the paperwhites into out-of-season bloom.

Perhaps all beauty is criminal. One could make that argument.
No one means to be mean, only kindness doesn't pay.

I've already betrayed the moths for garish butterflies.
As at the confluence of two rivers, one languid, one all hurtling speed...

Underwater it's hard to hear the ringing of the phone.

How Was It We Were Caught

after James Agee

in nets of veins
in bars of bone
in skeins of skin
in dreams of home
in barbs of breath
in hooks of eyes
in rays of sun
in nerves' bright wire
in muscles' strength
in dregs of hope
in wear of work
in weathered love
in 100 proof
in the mojo pin
in his iron fist
in his tender hand
in the heart's millstone
in the turning blood
in fate's meshed gears
in muck and mud
between the teeth of life
and talons of death
tyranny and gift
of breath and breath and breath

How Was It We Were Caught (2)

after James Agee

that couple on the road

could no more slow
their hearts, slough
their fear
         than could you
doff your privilege, un-
lace the corset of skin
that cuts you to the quick

so here you are
in the thick of it
the sun-bleached air
the hard-scrabble beauty of the land
the scene meticulously blocked
who you are, how they must stand

caught

your courtesy curdles to self-contempt
help to hindrance, harm

you would not be the hawk
the hawk's red eye

yet here they are
your unintended quarry
your unintended prey
straining hard against
the urge to scream, to run

your heart breaking
that old confusion
charity and love

Ether Net Blues

clueless   and crew
less   so this is me
the things I buy   the things
I own   but why stress?
this trend's unbuck
able   being's corporate
friends are capital   the im
mediate's gone   for good

c'mon   don't cry   idiot chile
life's a bubble   a globe
of snow   an enterprise
zone   and so much safer now
(select emoticon for smile)
for latch-key kids and ghosts

who needs the world?
who needs the soul?
old hat   bowler   fedora
you'd only look silly
the butt of some pimp's
joke   so bite the bullet   choke
on doubt   if you must
but spout no goose
girl manifestos   cuz no one loves
a hater   chile (select emoticon
for smile)   anesthetize   press play

The Wreck: Falling Under, Not Rising Above

after Eleanor Wilner

On the Doomsday clock, five minutes left to go—
caffeine rush, traffic jam, road rage, scandal, scams—
if you want to get to heaven better take it slow.

The pedal's to the metal though no one knows
just where we're headed. Today Iraq, tomorrow Iran...
On the Doomsday clock, five minutes left to go.

North Korea, India, Pakistan, holy Jerusalem all ready to blow,
You'd think we'd learn: two World Wars, Hiroshima, Vietnam.
If you want to get to heaven better take it slow.

But the genie won't go back into the bottle, or so
they say, and so we keep on running toward an-
nihilation. Five minutes left to go.

Remember 1989, how,
Cold War over and the Wall tumbled down,
it seemed like heaven, the world made new. For a second, time slowed.

But we're living in fast fast forward now
since the Towers fell and fear empowered a little man
to lead us to our Doom. Five minutes left to go.
Children playing up ahead. Pray to Heaven. Slow, slow.

Civil Disobedience

At the Intersection of Independence Avenue
and Capitol Plaza Southeast

The first time I got arrested
I felt free and powerful
like one bad-azzed
traffic officer disobeyer

especially as I stood there
hands cuffed behind my back
trying to chat up the young black cop
who couldn't risk telling me his name
though I was friendly and asked 3 times
and wouldn't let go of my arm
as if he thought I had some place to go,
as if I hadn't set the scene in motion,
hadn't left him no choice,
forced him to arrest me.

And they could take away
my belt, my shoelaces,
my diamond earring,
and keep me bound
one wrist to the wall
cold and by myself for hours

but what has any of that
to do with freedom?

Gun Rant

Virginia Tech, April 16, 2007

this is not about hunting,
this is not about sport,
this is not about your god-
forsaken constitutional right
to bear arms...

this is about lost
little boys, scared
little boys, angry
little boys and the lost,
scared, angry little boy-
men they become...

this is not about rights,
this is not about freedom,
this is not about the rule
of law or the common good...

this is about violence in our homes,
violence in our streets,
violence—senseless, bloody—in our schools...

this is not about hunting,
this is not about sport,
this is not about your god-
forsaken constitutional right
to bear arms...

this is not about self-preservation...

this is about lost
little boys, scared
little boys, angry
little boys and the lost,
scared, angry little
men they become...

this is about the lunatic fringe,
the armed militias of the militant right,
bedroom bruisers, skinheads and homethugs,
self-serving, spineless politicians
who court our votes with boldface lies
but won't say "boo" to the NRA…

this is about mayhem in our homes,
murder in our streets,
massacres—senseless, bloody—in our schools…

so here we stand,
lost scared angry
little children in the face
of so much death
on our own soil,
as if no one had told us
there's a war going on
and tolled the dead each day,
as if we didn't know
what guns, what bombs are for.

The Green Revolution

after the trenches were emptied
after the killing was done
after the sky over London
no longer rained nitrogen bombs
after the masters of war
had tallied up profits and loss
they trained their sights on farmers
here's nitrogen for your crops

after the chimneys were quiet
after Dresden burned
after a little boy's tantrum
after a fat man's yawn
after such death and destruction
on such an inhuman scale
they trained their sights on insects
nerve agents strafing our fields

after the alga bloom
after the reddening tide
after the vast dead zones
after whole fisheries died
after the blight of raw sewage
industrial and medical waste
after screening this muck from our water
rather than bury or incinerate

from the cities of the north and the east
from the captains of industry
comes sludge for the struggling farmer
good fertilizer and totally free
and the corporations fund the research
and the corporations fund the laws
and the corporations fund
and the corporations fund

and we eat and eat their wars

Jokers Wild and One-Eyed Jacks

each of us, islands—
why else red dye's daily run
scarcely touches us.

plates heave, volcanoes
blow—we are not moved.

what, heart, would you ask—
that we bleed with the bleeding,
die with the dying?

someone must survive,
praise instead of mourn.

heart, what would you ask?
some mad, impossible task—
reconfiguring

bit by broken bit
first world, cosmic egg?

yoked to so many
how'd we ever move or breathe?
interdependence—

what precarious
balance that implies,

such a fragile thread,
the cobweb casually swept
from the far corner...

but our lives make sense,
a just God loves us.

some reap the whirlwind;
others draw untroubled lives,
choices what to buy.

who said life was fair?
play the hand you're dealt.

heart, please, lift your eyes.
don't forsake the human face,
though you die of shame.

Meditation on a Theme Suggested by
Dr. Trellou Joseph Pond

How would it feel to really love your neighbor,
your neighbor who worships a stranger god?
What if your god allowed that man to prosper—

no plagues, no holy wars, no sanctioned slaughter
of first born sons? Could such a god be God?
How would it feel to really love your neighbor?

Will the salt of holiness have lost its savor
when no longer underwritten by the blood
of lambs, infidels, martyrs? If we prosper,

if we be long upon this earth brother
to brother, is God then obsolete? Or would
God dwell among us—familiar, stranger, neighbor?

Between our fallings-short and strivings-for
yawned an abyss so fell we needed God,
a cobbled ladder in order to cohere, let alone to prosper.

But if *they* were always *us* the terrible strangers—
attending angels, wrathful, jealous gods?
How would it feel to really love your neighbor?
To love your self? To reverence life? To prosper?

Blind Girl Grunt:
The Selected Blues Lyrics

While under contract to other record labels, Bob Dylan and Janis Ian contributed tracks to Broadside magazine's folk music compilations using the aliases Blind Boy Grunt and Blind Girl Grunt respectively.

Gone Courtin' Blues

I ain't much to look at,
But my heart is true and kind;

I know I ain't that much to look at,
But my heart is true and kind;

If it's lovin' you say you're after,
Well, honey, I'm the lovin' kind.

My purse is lean and windy,
But I got riches of my own;

I said my purse is lean and windy,
But I got riches of my own;

And if you'll be my lover, baby,
I'll give you kingdom, crown, and throne.

I'm no stranger to the blues, babe,
Cain't count the nights I've cried alone;

Said I'm no stranger to the blues, babe,
I've got the blues deep in my bones;

So if you need some understandin', honey,
You know I'll listen all night long.

I ain't no work of art, Mama,
But could you touch my soul and mind;

I know I ain't no Mona Lisa, Mama,
But could you glimpse my soul and mind,

Better git on your Ray-Bans, Mama,
'Cause my light will stone you blind.

Circadian Rhythm Blues

I been stayin' up all night and sleepin' half the day
I been stayin' up all night and sleepin' half the day
Don't ask me how I'm doin', I got nothin' to say.

If I had someone to love me I'd be in bed by half past ten
If I had someone to love me I'd be in bed by half past ten
Instead I'm stayin' up all night just searchin' for a friend.

There's an achin' in my head, but I'm voodooed by this screen
There's an achin' in my head, but I been voodooed by this screen
But all I'm so busy doin' don't mount to a hill a beans.

I need a woman's touch to slake my thirsty skin
I need a woman's sweet sweet touch to soothe my achin' skin
That this life don't afford a remedy is a cryin' doggone sin.

I fixed a box of brownies and ate them all las' night
Fixed myself a box of brownies and I ate them all las' night
All the sleep that I been losin I swear I'm gainin' back in weight.

Each day a resolution to take care of myself
Each day another resolution to take good care of myself
But what the hell does it matter, either way life ends in death.

I need soft arms to rock me, a sweet tongue in my mouth
Said I need soft arms to rock me, a sweet tongue in my mouth
There's a banquet on the table, but, Lord, this chile's without.

Somethin's gotta give, but I don't even wanna try
I know somethin's gotta give, but I don't even wanna try
And if it wasn't so much trouble I know I'd jus' lay down and die.

Good Day, Sunshine, Blues

Life's mean sometime
No sun and rain for weeks

Life's sho nuff mean sometime
No sun and rain for six long weeks

Sometime a good day, Sunshine,
Is just havin' more pans than leaks.

Life's mean sometime
Got dogbit by my own bitch

Life's downright mean sometime
I been dogbit by my own sweet little bitch

Sometime a good day, Darlin'
Is just shovelin' the same old shit.

Looked in the mirror this mornin'
And my reflection done up and gone

My company's so bad
Lawd, my reflection done up and gone

Sometime a good day, Sunshine,
Is bastin' in funk that's all your own.

Life's mean sometime
Sometime your own mama put you down

Life's sho nuff mean sometime
My own mama done put her baby down

Sometime a good day, Sunshine,
Is on the riverbottom drowned.

Dog-Man Blues

You can't stray from the yard
You can't come in from the cold

You can't stray from the yard
And you can't come in out the cold

They got you runnin' on a choke chain
They got you pacin' the threshold

You can't run with the pack
And they won't let you hunt alone

You can't run with the pack
And they don't 'low you hunt alone

Man give you a rag to sleep on
For hunger some lonesome bone

Don't bite the hand that feed you
Don't look a gift horse in the mouth

Don't bite the hand that feed you
Don't look a gift horse in the mouth

Take affection where it come
Forgive the out-a-nowhere kick of wrath

Revelation Blues

*For who or what is appointed to heal or mediate the "stricken" may just
as well be a gust of wind, a ghost, a book, an animal, a leaf, or a gesture.*
—Daniel Deardorff, *The Other Within*

Winds gotta' blow sometime
Unholy ghosts have got to roam

Hard winds gotta' blow sometime
Even unholy ghosts need a home

Sometime even the devil turn his back upon me
Sometime God's own angels ring my phone

Sometime not one book
Has got a single word for me

Sometime not one book
Has got one lousy word for me

The leaves turn brown & scatter
Dogs howl their witless sympathy

Sometime it don't mean nothin'
Sometime it mean most everything

Said sometime it don't mean nothin'
Sometime it mean everything

One look, one touch, one gesture
Opens the wound whence healing springs

Jay-Walkin' Blues

You got to stop on the red
You gots to move when the light turns green

You got to stop on the red
You gots to move along on green

You got to color in their lines, Lord
Or call down trouble like you never seen

Makes no difference if you're a hero
Or headed for a life of crime

Makes no difference if you're a hero
Or hellbent on a life of crime

Once you step across that line, man
You're gonna be lookin' at hard time

You got to walk the straight & narrow
Cleave to the middle of the road

You gots to walk it straight & narrow
Hold the middle of the road

Stray one iota left or right, Jack
& you done violated code.

Excuse my different eyes
Excuse my rough & tattered coat

Please excuse these eyes, ya'll
Pardon this rough & tattered coat

But if you're guardin' somethin' precious
You needs some dragons and a moat

The kingdom ain't for everyone
That's what the Bible say

You know the kingdom ain't for everyone
That's what my Good Book say

But if you wanna get a foretaste
Look up & meet this beggar's gaze

Less Than Greater Than Blues

Good morning, Mr. Charlie,
Can you spare a girl a dime?

Right fine morning, Mr. Charlie,
Can you please spare a girl a dime?

Mr. Charlie rush on pass me
Like his own life was on the line.

Black man's less than white man;
Blind man's less than that.

You know black man's less than white man;
Blind man's even less than that.

But in the sight of a good woman,
He's no less a man for that.

I had a lovely sister;
Her eyes were blear and vague as mine.

I had one lovely sister,
Eyes as blear and vague as mine.

Seem like every sorry no-count joker
Lined up to waste that woman's time.

Woman's less than man;
Blind woman's less than anything.

Tell me woman's less than man;
Blind woman's worse than anything.

Lord, folks act like they can't see me;
They's gonna hear me when I sing.

Song of Her Dark Hair

Demolition / Prayer

When they went
to close the coffin
grief cried out
fit to break
the most obdurate heart,

and it was then,
turning to my friend,
I blessed my lonely life
and (rightly so)
was soberly chastised:

living alone won't
spare you anything,
surely you know that;
you will still love, Constance,
and love bears loss.

Thoughts of this woman
who has loved one other
longer than I've been alive—
how will she survive?
What will she do with his name?—

crash against me hard
whooshing out all my breath.
But against death what other
stay than love?
Shove back this stone

from the grave of my heart,
erect a beautiful palace
within its pulsing walls,
and let two live there a long long time
before the wrecking ball.

So Much Depends / Upon

so much depends
upon

the Ohio
River

confluence
     and tributary
flood plain
     and drainage basin

the Monongahela
     and the Allegheny
the Muskinghum and
     the Kanawha
and their sweet diminutives

the Beaver and the Duck
the Big and Little Sandy
the Miami Great and small

the Guyandotte
     and the Scioto
the Green and the Salt
not to be confused with
     the Saline

the Tennessee
     the Cache
     the Licking
          best of all

pirates and keelboats
Hey, ho, the boatman row
sailin' on the river
on the Ohio!

freedom over Jordan
    Eliza, babe in arms,
                hopscotching
        jack-in-the-box
                          ice floes

unquenchable thirst
the many hungers

      channel catfish
          longnose gar
    silver carp
        skipjack herring

and let's not forget
    the breath-stopping
        heart-
            dropping
before-hard-logic-of-locks-and-dams
              26-feet-in-a-2-mile-stretch

                          Falls

the song of her dark hair

After the Flood

In this new place one awakes
to apocalyptic thunderstorms,
the sky a troubling green, high winds,
and rain hammering down and down.
Our usually timid tortie sleeps curled
serenely on an upholstered dining chair,
while her bad-ass fatty brother
flattens himself against the floor
and like some delicate pastry batter,
gingerly folds himself beneath the bed.
Sure that I can't fit, I wait out the storm
huddled under a blanket on top of the bed.
Meanwhile, my lover braves the storm,
though I had earnestly entreated her to stay.

Later in the day we begin to get the news:
seventy-five minutes, six inches of rain,
the city's sewer system overwhelmed,
the University closed, 50 there rescued by boat,
an animal shelter flooded, at least 12 animals dead,
nearly four feet of water in the main library
basement, windows blown, extensive damage,
closed till further notice, at least till after Labor Day,
and just one block down our little street
cars halfway under water. My beloved drove through blinding rain;
I dozed with cats after sending up
what might have passed as prayer.
The sky brewed a troubling green;
rain hammered down and down.

Parody / Prayer

Let us lie here you and I
And scarcely move or breathe a sigh
As if we were corpses frozen in lovebed
By the blowing of Pompeii.
Let you rest your lips on mine
While outside the morning breaks,
Swishing its tail against the windowpane
Like a big contented sloppy dog.
What would be the point to move?
What would be the point of speech?
Love speaks best without a tongue.
Then let us lie but never lie.
O Lord, hear my prayer:
Beneath one hearth we share one breath;.
Inside two lives we bear one death;
Save us from the time of trial.

Oh, Lovergirl, what is it?
Little Poppy came to visit!

The sun set like aubergines.
We walked beneath the fragrant trees.
Truth to tell, no sun but rain,
Still we found the Quiet Garden.
The treetop road closed in darkness.
Afraid, you wanted to turn back.
Your hands held the wheel,
But it was my will that drove us on
Until a gate barred our way.
Repeatedly I apologized,
Backing down that narrow road,
Looking for a place to turn.
Let's go back to the Quiet Garden.
Let's look over the Big Prairie.
There will be time, there will be time,
To walk along the canopies of trees,

To find a place to find our knees,
To kneel and be blessed, to heal and be whole:
The peace of God be with you.

Oh, Lovergirl, what is it?
Little Poppy came to visit!

"Honey, do we live in the 'hood?"
"Yes," you replied, happy I had finally asked.
After six years gone the Red Giraffe still knew you;
It lowered its head and grazed from your palm.
Birdsong at dawn, lullabies at noon,
Sirens at evening, and compline by moon,
The Sisters of Mercy nestle like doves,
Calm then frenzied, frenzied then calm.
Cats scratch at the door desperate to be fed,
Filled, they butt against our hands compelling love.
They weave themselves around our legs like fog wreathing trees;
Our legs grow indistinct. And then it's time to sleep.
All day they sleep; they lie and do not move.
Their bellies no longer trouble them;
Their claws are bloody but their consciences are clean.
Oh, Lord, deliver me not into the claws of Septimus.

Oh, Lord, deliver us not into the mouths of evangelicals.
Deliver us not into the milky spit of fundamentalists
Who think to curse two women holding hands on the street.
May their spit dry up like desert arroyos.
May their spit grow weak as an old man's semen.
May they choke on their own crooked curdled curses.
Let us remain here; do not deliver us,
For we have already been delivered and are home.
Still the mailman grudges us tidings of our loved ones,
Withholds our packages, serves us only duns.
Oh, Lord, deliver the mailman from his grudgingness,
Deliver unto him daily love letters and passionate kisses nightly;
Soften his heart and make it light as airmail parchment.
It is no matter. It is only matter.
The spirit of communion has chosen us.

The peace of God be with you. And also with you.
Let us lie here, still and burning,
Like a picture painted by Michelangelo.
No, like a sketch he works on daily:
Drawing one line, erasing another,
Adding a swath of shading, a wash of holy light.

Ephemeroptera Hymn

composed on a line by Pablo Neruda

In tight green buds, the harvests' sweet goodbyes.
Remember Bradford pears and dogwoods singing on the street!
When I die, I want your hands upon my eyes.

One minute snow, the next petals, falling soft as sighs,
and you and I, Imagine! once so cold beneath our sheets.
In tight green buds, the harvests' sweet goodbyes.

In all our firsts, my love, did we not surmise
Sun-drunk desire rounding to replete?
When I die, I want your hands upon my eyes.

But stay, let's not go in until the last light dies.
Tireless as birdsong may our days repeat repeat.
In tight green buds, the harvests' sweet goodbyes.

And, yes, within this beauty creeps a terror I can't disguise.
Is knowledge of the scythe borne in the wheat?
When I die, I want your hands upon my eyes.

My wife, my all, let us join in the dance of the one-day-flies.
Neither from love, nor life, nor loss let us retreat.
In tight green buds, the harvests' sweet goodbyes.
When I die, I want your hands upon my eyes.

Advent

A newborn child comes crying into the world,
And you forget everything: the pain-
Ful hours of labor, the arduous journey
To an inhospitable town, gravity's
Insistent aching pull; the prostrate soul
Stands bolt upright and every nerve and cell
Waits at attention. And whether that face,
So unprecedented, precious, perfect, here,
Stops your heart or makes it beat again
After years of failure and arrest, it's hard
To say. Time slows; history unravels:
No more Pilates, Caesars, Herods, Pharaohs;
Oppression, exile, torture, death, taxes.
This first moment of mutual regarding
Remembers time, and God is speaking light
Into the world. And again and still it is morning
And God is breathing life into mere dust.
Tender as a new leaf, radiant as the sun:
Greedily you drink him in; greedily he drinks you in.
This, you know, is love, is all, the end
And the beginning, the continual present: now
And always. After a lifetime of crippling doubt
Certainty lies sleeping in your arms.
You could not help but to be mesmerized.
But even now some hapless messenger,
Winging his way toward you with vital news,
Frays the nether border of the spell.
You feel or think you feel some disturbance
In the air. You hear or think your hear...what?...
In the far-off distance. You look up, shifting your eyes
Away from the sleeping child, and just like that
The moment breaks. And though only seconds
Have passed, returning, your gaze finds love's first face gone.
Again and again you look; only traces remain.
When the messenger arrives and speaks his piece,
You will take up the child, grown stranger year

By year, and flee into the desert, shot
Like an arrow from history's brutal bow.
Some days you'll scarcely know the child teaching
In the temple, hammering a nail, sassing his dam.
And how he hates the way you look at him,
Stare at him, he'd say. But how explain
You're conjuring a vision, remembering a dream?
Sometimes of course you forget, but you never forget.
Some days you're sure the longing will kill you.
Some days you're sure the longing saves your life.
You wish that it would end and you fear that end.
But it doesn't end. Not even when he hangs from a cross,
Or briefly lies lifeless in a tomb.
Not even when he rises from the dead
And dwells, utterly changed, among us
Does it end. It is always only the beginning.
I am in you, and you are in me.
Take, eat this bread, my body broken for you.
Now it's been years since you've met a stranger,
Seeing in each face an intimate glimpse of God.

Grace Notes

always & everywhere

A Child of Hamelin

after Rachel Smith's "The Pied Piper"

She wants to live
somewhere
not a body,
some way not
in daily check
to biology's decay.
Once she thought
another's body,
later, another's mind;
now she thinks she feels
most free, most safe
inside the bars of song

Facing Silence

after Walter Martin & Paloma Munoz

Aria angel ascend the crystal air;
Rend anguish to patience, patience to prayer.
There is no portentous star, no trumpet's blare,
No heavenly hosts, no hallelujah choir.
Lonely night. Frost bite. The sun has lost its fire.
Adamant, at whose bidding, at whose desire
Have you fallen with the snow? No listener
Hastens, hearkens, nears. Pull your snow pelt closer.
Perhaps your songs will melt the heart of God, pure
Diamond inattentive brilliance. Sleepers stir
Witched by the strange snow light, but do not wake. Fare
Well unheralded herald, chill messenger.
You can only save yourself. Tear, prisoner,
Pierce with fatal note illusion's lung. Fierce, ascend.

About the Author

Constance Merritt was born in Pine Bluff, Arkansas, and educated at the Arkansas School for the Blind in Little Rock. She is the author of three previous poetry collections. She lives in Louisville, KY with her wife, Maria Accardi.

Headmistress Press Books

Lovely - Lesléa Newman
Teeth & Teeth - Robin Reagler
How Distant the City - Freesia McKee
Shopgirls - Marissa Higgins
Riddle - Diane Fortney
When She Woke She Was an Open Field - Hilary Brown
God With Us - Amy Lauren
A Crown of Violets - Renée Vivien tr. Samantha Pious
Fireworks in the Graveyard - Joy Ladin
Social Dance - Carolyn Boll
The Force of Gratitude - Janice Gould
Spine - Sarah Caulfield
Diatribe from the Library - Farrell Greenwald Brenner
Blind Girl Grunt - Constance Merritt
Acid and Tender - Jen Rouse
Beautiful Machinery - Wendy DeGroat
Odd Mercy - Gail Thomas
The Great Scissor Hunt - Jessica K. Hylton
A Bracelet of Honeybees - Lynn Strongin
Whirlwind @ Lesbos - Risa Denenberg
The Body's Alphabet - Ann Tweedy
First name Barbie last name Doll - Maureen Bocka
Heaven to Me - Abe Louise Young
Sticky - Carter Steinmann
Tiger Laughs When You Push - Ruth Lehrer
Night Ringing - Laura Foley
Paper Cranes - Dinah Dietrich
On Loving a Saudi Girl - Carina Yun
The Burn Poems - Lynn Strongin
I Carry My Mother - Lesléa Newman
Distant Music - Joan Annsfire
The Awful Suicidal Swans - Flower Conroy
Joy Street - Laura Foley
Chiaroscuro Kisses - G.L. Morrison
The Lillian Trilogy - Mary Meriam
Lady of the Moon - Amy Lowell, Lillian Faderman, Mary Meriam
Irresistible Sonnets - ed. Mary Meriam
Lavender Review - ed. Mary Meriam

Made in the USA
Middletown, DE
10 December 2020